A FULL MOON is RISING

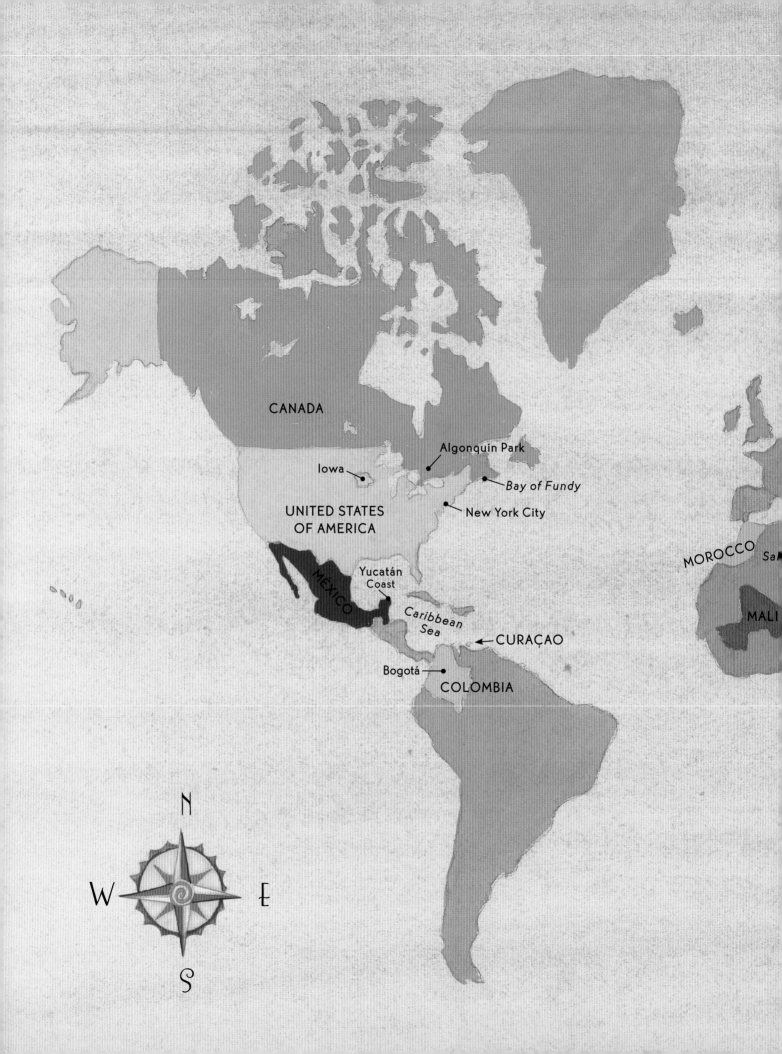

TURKEY

Ephesus

ISRAEL

Haifa

Pushkar

INDIA

CHINA

Hong Kong

Broome

SOUTH
AFRICA

Cape
Town

AUSTRALIA

To my friend and co-host of the Poetry Blast, Barbara Genco —M.S.

For my nieces, Abigail Cairns and Charlotte Dukes, always with love —J.C.

A FULL MOON IS RISING

poems by MARILYN SINGER

pictures by JULIA CAIRNS

Lee & Low Books Inc. | New York

ACKNOWLEDGMENTS

Thanks to Steve Aronson, Shawn Davis, Rebecca Kai Dotlich, Susan Pearson, earth science teacher Sara Schenker,
my wonderful editor Louise May, and the great folks at Lee & Low.

LEE & LOW BOOKS Inc., 95 Madison Avenue, New York, NY 10016 · leeandlow.com

Manufactured in Malaysia by Tien Wah Press

Book design by Kimi Weart · Book production by The Kids at Our House · The text is set in Martin Gothic · The illustrations are rendered in watercolor

(hc) 10 9 8 7 6 5 4

(pb) 10 9 8 7 6 5 4 3 2

First Edition

Library of Congress Cataloging-in-Publication Data

Singer, Marilyn.

A full moon is rising : poems by Marilyn Singer ; pictures by Julia Cairns. — 1st ed.

p. cm.

ISBN 978-1-60060-364-8 (hardcover : alk. paper) · ISBN 978-1-62014-196-0 (pb)

1. Moon—Juvenile poetry. I. Cairns, Julia. II. Title.

PS3569.I546F85 2011   811'.54—dc22   2010034693

MIX
Paper from responsible sources
FSC www.fsc.org FSC® C012700

AUTHOR'S SOURCES

MOON ASTRONOMY AND SUPERSTITION

Brueton, Diana. *Many Moons*. New York: Simon & Schuster, 1991.

Carroll, Robert T. "Full moon and lunar effects." *The Skeptic's Dictionary*. Last updated July 30, 2010. http://skepdic.com/fullmoon.html.

Kriebel, Matthew. "Urban Astronomy—Seeing the Skies in Light Polluted Areas." Ezine Articles, September 4, 2008. http://ezinearticles.com/?Urban-Astronomy—Seeing-the-Skies-in-Light-Polluted-Areas&id=1468200.

Miles, Kathy. "Moon Watching." Starry Skies.com. http://starryskies.com/The_sky/events/lunar-2003/moonwatching.html.

Moon Connection.com. http://www.moonconnection.com/.

Phillips, Dr. Tony. "Watch Out for the Harvest Moon." NASA, September 16, 2005. Last updated April 5, 2010. http://science.nasa.gov/science-news/science-at-nasa/2000/ast11sep_2/.

Ptak, Andy, and Gail Rohrback. "Ask an Astrophysicist." NASA Goddard Space Flight Center. Last updated August 16, 2010. http://imagine.gsfc.nasa.gov/docs/ask_astro/ask_an_astronomer.html.

Simon, Seymour. *The Moon*. New York: Simon & Schuster, 2003.

LUNAR FESTIVALS

Fitzgerald, Waverly. *School of the Seasons*. http://www.schooloftheseasons.com/.

"Harvest Festivals from Around the World." Harvest Festivals.net. http://www.harvestfestivals.net/harvestfestivals.htm.

"Mid-Autumn Festival." China Voc.com. http://www.chinavoc.com/festivals/Midautumn.htm.

"Pushkar Fair." Pushkar: The Sacred Place. http://www.pushkar-camel-fair.com/pushkar-fair.html.

Rich, Tracey R. "Sukkot." Judaism 101. http://www.jewfaq.org/holiday5.htm.

"Sukkah." *Wikipedia*. Last modified August 14, 2010. http://en.wikipedia.org/wiki/Sukkah.

Yiu, Julian. "Mid-Autumn Festival: An Introduction." China the Beautiful. http://www.chinapage.com/Moon/moon-intro.html.

LUNAR ECLIPSE AND MOON ILLUSIONS

Davis, Shawn. "Letters From Mali: Bringing Back the Moon." Peace Corps: Paul D. Coverdell Worldwise Schools, November 1996. http://www.peacecorps.gov/wws/stories/stories.cfm?psid=99.

McCready, Don. "The Moon Illusion Explained." University of Wisconsin-Whitewater. Revised November 10, 2004. http://facstaff.uww.edu/mccreadd/.

Phillips, Dr. Tony. "Solstice Moon Illusion." NASA, June 16, 2008. Last updated April 5, 2010. http://science.nasa.gov/science-news/science-at-nasa/2008/16jun_moonillusion/.

———. "Summer Moon Illusion." NASA, June, 20, 2005. Last updated November 30, 2007. http://www.nasa.gov/vision/universe/watchtheskies/20jun_moonillusion.html.

Rivera, Larry. "Staircase to the Moon." About.com: Australia/New Zealand Travel. http://goaustralia.about.com/od/wa/ss/staircase-to-the-moon.htm.

TIDES AND THE BAY OF FUNDY

Cooley, Keith. "Moon Tides: How the Moon Affects Ocean Tides." Keith's Moon Page, 2002. http://home.hiwaay.net/~krcool/Astro/moon/moontides/.

Ferguson, George. "Highest Tides: The Tides." Bay of Fundy.com. http://www.bayoffundy.com/tides.aspx.

"What causes high tide and low tide? Why are there two tides each day?" How Stuff Works. http://science.howstuffworks.com/environmental/earth/geophysics/tide-cause.htm.

CORAL SPAWNING AND BIRD MIGRATION

Lincoln, Frederick C. "Migration of Birds, Circular 16." U.S. Fish and Wildlife Service, 1935. Revised 1979 by Steven R. Peterson, revised 1998 by John L. Zimmerman. http://www.fws.gov/birds/documents/MigrationofBirdsCircular.pdf.

"Moon-Watching: Studying Birds that Migrate." Chipper Woods Bird Observatory. http://www.wbu.com/chipperwoods/photos/moon.htm.

Reefcare Foundation, Coral Spawning. http://www.reefcare.org/.

The Nature Writers of Texas Blog; "Bird Migration Is An Amazing Event," blog entry by Ro Wauer, April 13, 2003. http://texasnature.blogspot.com/2003/04/bird-migration-is-amazing-event-ro.html.

TEMPLE OF ARTEMIS

Hayes, Holly. "Artemis of Ephesus (Ephesian Artemis)." Sacred Destinations, June 2007. http://www.sacred-destinations.com/turkey/ephesus-artemis.htm.

"Temple of Artemis." Kusadasi.biz. http://www.kusadasi.biz/historical-places/temple-of-artemis.html.

GARAVITO'S CRATER

Astronomy Radar Blog; "The lunar crater of Julio Garavito Armero," blog entry by Thilo Hanisch Luque, February 24, 2010. http://astroradar.blogspot.com/2010/02/lunar-crater-of-julio-garavito-armero.html.

Today in Astronomy Blog; "January 5: Julio Garavito Armero," blog entry by Lunar Mark, January 5, 2009. http://todayinastronomy.blogspot.com/2009/01/january-5-julio-garavito-armero.html.

PHOBOS / MARS

Knight, J. D. "Phobos." Sea and Sky: The Sky. http://www.seasky.org/solar-system/mars-phobos.html.

| New Moon | Waxing Crescent | First Quarter | Waxing Gibbous | Full Moon | Waning Gibbous | Third Quarter | Waning Crescent |

Our earth has just one moon, its only natural satellite. Cold, dusty, rocky, and dry, the moon is, on average, nearly 240,000 miles (approximately 384,000 kilometers) from us. It does not give off its own light. What we see as lunar light is really sunlight reflecting off the moon's surface. It takes twenty-eight days for the moon to orbit the earth. As it orbits, the moon's angle changes in relation to the earth and the sun, and we see its different phases: new moon (dark phase), waxing crescent, first quarter, waxing gibbous, full moon, waning gibbous, third quarter, waning crescent, and back to new.

All around the world, people and other living things are affected by the changing phases of the moon. But perhaps the most celebrated phase is the full moon. Sailors set out to sea on the high tides it causes. Insects and migrating birds are guided by its brilliant light. Families dance, sing, and feast at full moon festivals, while traders buy and sell camels. Corals reproduce, wolves howl, and children dream of being astronauts on full moon nights.

So come along on a lunar journey to see the many ways we welcome our wondrous full moon.

| New Moon | Waxing Crescent | First Quarter | Waxing Gibbous | Full Moon | Waning Gibbous | Third Quarter | Waning Crescent |

Broadway Moon

New York City, USA

It waits behind skyscrapers,
a brilliant actor in the wings,
ready for its monthly debut.
On the sidewalk, an audience of one
watches and silently applauds
when it grandly appears.

High Tide

Bay of Fundy, Canada

Sail on a Saturday.
Sail on a Monday.
You'll find the highest tides of all
here, in the Bay of Fundy.

Sail at a new moon.
Sail at a full.
Waters spring up to their peak
to heed the lunar pull.

One hundred billion tonnes of water
in and out the bay.
One hundred billion tonnes of water
two times every day.

Sail in December
or sail in June.
Set out on a high tide.
Always thank the moon.